Essential
THAI
COOKBOOK

Essential THAI COOKBOOK

50 Classic Recipes, with Step-by-Step Photographs

Edited by Heather Thomas

COURAGE BOOKS

AN IMPRINT OF RUNNING PRESS
PHILADELPHIA • LONDON

Printed in Hong Kong

9 8 7 6 5 4 3 2 1

Digit on the right indicates the number of this printing

Library of Congress Cataloging-in-Publication Number
97-77961

ISBN 0-7624-0380-2

Designed and produced by SP Creative Design
Editor: Heather Thomas
Art Director: Al Rockall
Designer: Rolando Ugolini

Acknowledgements

Special photography: James Murphy
Step-by-step photography: GGS Photographics
Food preparation: Janet Smith and Dawn Stock

This book may be ordered by mail from the publisher.
But try your bookstore first!

Published by Courage Books, an imprint of
Running Press Book Publishers
125 South Twenty-second Street
Philadelphia, Pennsylvania 19103-4399

Notes

1. Standard spoon measurements are used in all recipes.

2. Eggs should be large unless otherwise stated.

3. Whole milk should be used unless otherwise stated.

4. Fresh herbs should be used unless otherwise stated.
If unavailable, use dried herbs as an alternative, but halve the
quantities stated.

5. Ovens should be preheated to the specified temperature.
If using a convection oven, follow the manufacturer's
instructions for adjusting the time and the temperature.

CONTENTS

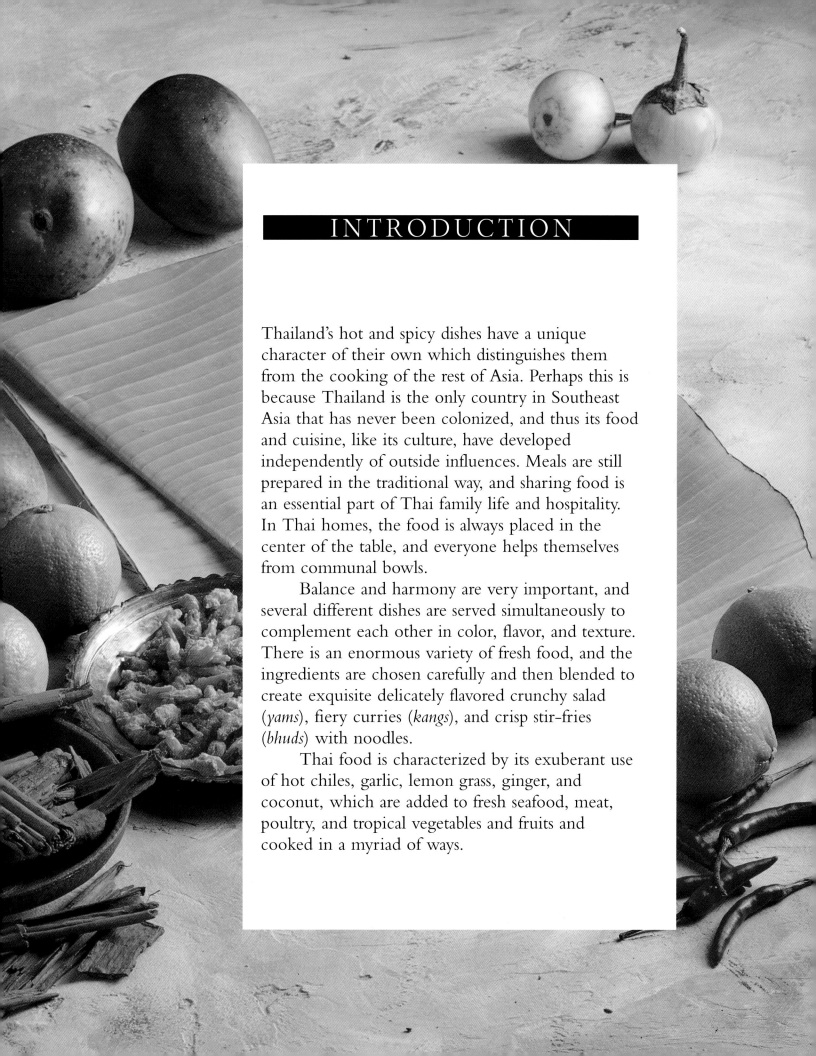

INTRODUCTION

Thailand's hot and spicy dishes have a unique character of their own which distinguishes them from the cooking of the rest of Asia. Perhaps this is because Thailand is the only country in Southeast Asia that has never been colonized, and thus its food and cuisine, like its culture, have developed independently of outside influences. Meals are still prepared in the traditional way, and sharing food is an essential part of Thai family life and hospitality. In Thai homes, the food is always placed in the center of the table, and everyone helps themselves from communal bowls.

Balance and harmony are very important, and several different dishes are served simultaneously to complement each other in color, flavor, and texture. There is an enormous variety of fresh food, and the ingredients are chosen carefully and then blended to create exquisite delicately flavored crunchy salad (*yams*), fiery curries (*kangs*), and crisp stir-fries (*bhuds*) with noodles.

Thai food is characterized by its exuberant use of hot chiles, garlic, lemon grass, ginger, and coconut, which are added to fresh seafood, meat, poultry, and tropical vegetables and fruits and cooked in a myriad of ways.

Thai food takes quite a long time to prepare but the cooking methods are usually very simple and quick. You can prepare a meal in advance and then cook it literally in minutes, making it an extremely healthy fast food.

Bamboo shoots

These are the tender young shoots of the bamboo plant. They are widely used in stir-fried dishes, and can be bought in cans in most supermarkets and specialist food stores and delicatessens.

Banana leaves

Some foods are baked or steamed in banana leaves, notably fish, dumplings, and glutinous rice (sticky rice). If you cannot obtain fresh leaves, you can substitute oiled aluminum foil instead.

Bean curd

Made from puréed soy beans, bean curd is high in protein, low in fat, and very nutritious. It has a soft texture and may be sliced or cubed. It can be purchased fresh or vacuum-packed from oriental stores, health food stores, and some supermarkets.

Chiles

Thai chiles are small, narrow, and tapering and may be red or green. In spite of their size—they are seldom more than two to three inches in length, and the tiny "birdseye" chiles are no more than half an inch long—they are extremely hot and fiery, and great care should be taken when cutting them as the seeds can burn your skin. Always wash your hands immediately after handling chiles and avoid contact with the eyes. They can also be purchased dried.

The Thais love chiles, believing that they cool the body and stimulate the appetite, bringing balance and harmony to their food.

Cilantro

The leaves and roots of this herb help to give Thai food its distinctive flavor. It resembles flat-leaf parsley in appearance, but here any similarity ends as it has a very intense, almost spicy flavor. In Thailand, cilantro roots are usually crushed with garlic and then used to flavor meat dishes and curries. The leaves are used universally to garnish every conceivable kind of savory dish.

Coconut cream and milk

When added to spicy dishes and hot curries, coconut cream and milk create a distinctive creamy texture. You can make your own coconut milk by boiling fresh or desiccated coconut in milk and then squeezing out the juice (see page 111) or you can buy it ready-made. Coconut cream is the thick liquid that forms on the surface of coconut milk when it is chilled in the refrigerator. You can skim it off to use in a variety of dishes. It is also available in cartons and cans. Remember that when you are cooking with coconut milk, you must take care that it does not curdle. When bringing it to a boil, stir constantly, and never cover the wok or saucepan while it is cooking.

Curry pastes

These are made traditionally in a mortar by pounding together fresh herbs and hot spices, especially chiles, lemon grass, lime leaves, ginger, garlic, and cilantro. They may be red or green, depending on the color of the chiles used. Western cooks can substitute a blender or electric grinder to make lighter work of the pounding.

Eggplants

Thai eggplants are small and green with a crunchy texture. They are sometimes stuffed and deep-fried, or may be eaten raw in salads.

Galanga

This mellow pine-flavored root is the cousin of root ginger and a member of the ginger family. It is prepared in a similar fashion to fresh ginger: by peeling and crushing. It is often used in its powdered form—*laos*. A slice of fresh galanga is roughly equivalent to half a teaspoon of *laos* powder.

Ginger

Ginger is of Indian or Chinese origin but it is firmly established as an essential ingredient in Thai cookery. It is always used fresh rather than dried, and is peeled and then chopped or crushed before cooking. The ginger we buy in the West is often fibrous and quite dry in texture, but fresh ginger in Thailand is green and tender and highly flavored.

Glutinous rice

Also known as "sticky rice," this fragrant short-grain rice sticks together when cooked. It is used in both sweet and savory dishes, and may also be ground into flour. It is usually cooked by steaming in banana leaves.

Lemon grass (*takrai*)

The aromatic bulbous root end of lemon grass looks rather like a small, slim leek and is used sliced, crushed, or chopped in a wide range of Thai dishes, especially curries, soups, and salads. The stem end is added whole to spicy soups and curries, and it yields a strong lemon fragrance and flavor. Ground to a fine powder, it is known as *serai*; one teaspoon of powder is equivalent to one blade of fresh lemon grass.

Lime leaves

Strongly citrus flavored kaffir lime (*makrut*) leaves are used to flavor curries, soups, and many other dishes. If you cannot obtain these, you could substitute bay leaves but the flavor will be different.

Nam pla (fish sauce)

This is the most commonly used flavoring in Thai food and is added to nearly all savory dishes to accentuate the flavors of the other ingredients. It is made from salted anchovies and is quite salty and strongly flavored. Bottled *nam pla* is now sold in most supermarkets.

Oyster sauce

This bottled sauce, which is made from oysters and soy sauce, is used to flavor stir-fried meat, poultry, fish, and vegetable dishes.

Palm sugar

This heavy, strongly flavored, hard brown sugar is made from the sap of the coconut palm tree. If you cannot obtain it, you can use dark brown Barbados sugar instead.

Soy sauce

Made from fermented soy beans, soy sauce may be light or dark and is quite salty. It is added to many chicken and stir-fried dishes, especially noodles.

Tamarind

This acidic tropical fruit resembles a bean pod and is usually sold dried or pulped. Dried tamarind should be soaked in warm water for at least 10 minutes before cooking. It is then squeezed to extract the pulp, which is sieved with the soaking water. The fibrous material is discarded, and the tamarind juice can be boiled and stored, or added immediately to many dishes.

Vermicelli

There are two types of vermicelli: rice sticks (*sen mee*) and transparent noodles (*wun sen*). Rice sticks are dried noodles made from rice flour. They come in a range of widths, ranging from quite wide ribbon noodles to very thin, string-like ones, and may be deep-fried or soaked in water and then boiled. Transparent noodles are made from mung bean flour and are always soaked in water before cooking.

Wonton wrappers

These squares of wafer-thin noodle dough are made from flour, eggs, and water and can be bought fresh or frozen in a variety of sizes, although the most commonly used is 3 inches square. They are filled with delicious savory mixtures and then steamed or fried.

Cooking utensils

Most meals are cooked in a *wok*, a wide rounded shallow pan with a curved base, which is perfect for deep-frying, stir-frying and cooking curries and simmered dishes. The other most useful utensils are a large steamer (usually made of bamboo) and a granite mortar and pestle for grinding spices, pounding fresh herbs, and making curry pastes. You need strong muscles to use this and you may prefer to opt for an electric blender or grinder, which takes all the hard work out of pounding. Sharp knives are essential for all the chopping and preparation, as is a cleaver for cutting up meat and poultry.

SHRIMP SOUP

Meng tom yam kung

1½ pounds uncooked shrimp

9 cups water

6 small kaffir lime leaves

1 tablespoon chopped lemon grass

2 teaspoons nam pla (fish sauce)

⅓ cup fresh lime juice

4 tablespoons sliced cilantro leaves

3 tablespoons sliced scallions

1 red chile, seeded and sliced into
1-inch strips

salt and pepper

2 Pour the water into a large saucepan and bring to a boil. Add the lime leaves and chopped lemon grass, reduce the heat and simmer for 10 minutes. Add the nam pla and cook for a further 5 minutes.

3 Add the shrimp and lime juice to the pan and cook gently over a very low heat for a few minutes, until the shrimp become firm and turn a pale pink color.

1 Prepare the shrimp: shell them and remove the dark vein running along the back. Wash them under running water, drain and pat dry with absorbent paper towels. Set aside while you make the soup.

4 Add the sliced cilantro leaves, scallions, and red chile strips to the soup. Check the seasoning, adding salt and pepper if wished, and serve very hot in small bowls.

PREPARATION: 5 MINUTES
COOKING: 25 MINUTES
SERVES: 6

CHICKEN AND COCONUT SOUP

Kai tom kah

2 Strain the stock into a clean saucepan. Add the coconut milk, stirring until blended. Bring to a boil and then simmer gently over a low heat for 10 minutes.

3 Bone the chicken portions and remove the skin. Cut the meat into very thin slices.

4 Stir the lime juice, sliced chicken and brown sugar into the soup. Simmer for 2–3 minutes and then serve garnished with chiles and fresh basil leaves.

1 Bring the chicken stock, breast portions, onion, lemon grass, lime leaves, and ginger to a boil. Cover the pan and simmer for 40 minutes.

5 cups chicken stock
3 chicken breast portions
1 onion, finely chopped
3 stalks lemon grass, cut into 3 pieces and crushed
3 kaffir lime leaves
8 slices peeled root ginger
1½ cups coconut milk (see page 111)
juice of 1 lime
2 teaspoons brown sugar
2 fresh red chiles, seeded and chopped
a few basil leaves

PREPARATION: 15 MINUTES
COOKING: 1 HOUR
SERVES: 4–6

SHRIMP AND SQUID HOT SOUP

Tom yum kung lae pla muk

3   Add the prepared shrimp and squid to the pan and continue cooking gently over low heat for about 3–4 minutes until the shrimp turn pink and firm. Add a little *nam pla* to taste.

1   Clean and wash the squid, and pat dry with absorbent paper towels. Cut off the tentacles and chop into small pieces. Cut the body into thin rings. Set aside while you make the soup.

½ pound squid
7 cups chicken stock
6 kaffir lime leaves
1 stalk lemon grass, crushed
½ pound uncooked shrimp, shelled and deveined
nam pla (fish sauce), to taste
4 fresh green chiles, sliced into rounds
2 garlic cloves, minced
juice of 1 lime or lemon
salt and pepper
To garnish:
chopped cilantro leaves

PREPARATION: 15 MINUTES
COOKING: 15 MINUTES
SERVES: 4

2   Pour the chicken stock into a large saucepan and bring to a boil. Add the lime leaves and lemon grass, then reduce the heat and simmer gently for about 5 minutes.

4   Stir the green chiles into the soup. Mix together the garlic with the lime or lemon juice in a small bowl until well blended, and then stir into the soup. Adjust the seasoning if necessary, adding salt and pepper to taste. Pour the soup into 4 warmed individual serving bowls. Serve sprinkled with chopped cilantro.

FRIED WONTON

Geow grob

1 Put the ground pork in a small bowl with the chopped onion, garlic mixture and *nam pla*. Mix well together to combine all the ingredients to a thick paste.

2 Spread the wonton wrappers out on the work surface and put a teaspoon of the pork mixture in the centre of each wrapper.

3 Brush the edges of the wrappers with the egg yolk, and then fold the wrappers over to enclose the filling and make a triangular shape. Press the edges firmly together, sealing with more egg yolk if necessary.

½ pound ground pork
1 tablespoon finely chopped onion
2 teaspoons garlic mixture (see page 110)
½ tablespoon *nam pla* (fish sauce)
20 wonton wrappers (ones that are suitable for frying)
1 egg yolk
oil for deep-frying
To serve:
plum sauce or chile sauce (see page 110)

PREPARATION: 15 MINUTES
COOKING: 5–10 MINUTES
SERVES: 4–5

4 Heat the oil in a wok or large heavy-based skillet and fry the filled wonton, a few at a time, for about 5 minutes, until they are golden brown. Turn them over in the oil if necessary to brown both sides. Drain on absorbent paper towels and serve hot with plum sauce or chile sauce.

PORK ON SKEWERS

Satay

1 pound pork tenderloin
1 teaspoon salt
2 teaspoons brown sugar
1 teaspoon ground turmeric
1 teaspoon ground cilantro
1 teaspoon ground cumin
³/4 cup coconut milk (see page 111)
For the peanut sauce:
¹/2 cup roasted peanuts
1 teaspoon salt
1¹/4 cups coconut milk (see page 111)
2 teaspoons red curry paste (see page 111)
2 tablespoons sugar
¹/2 teaspoon lemon juice

2 Make the peanut sauce: grind the peanuts with the salt in a mortar until the mixture has the consistency of thick cream. Set aside.

3 Put half of the coconut milk in a saucepan with the curry paste. Heat gently for 3 minutes, stirring constantly. Stir in the creamed peanuts with the sugar, lemon juice, and the remaining coconut milk. Simmer gently for 20–30 minutes, stirring occasionally to prevent it sticking to the pan. Transfer to a bowl.

4 Thread the marinated pork on to oiled bamboo skewers and cook on a barbecue or under a hot broiler for 12–15 minutes, turning them several times and brushing frequently with the reserved coconut milk. Serve the kebobs with the peanut sauce.

1 Cut the pork into 2-inch long strips and place in a large bowl. Add the salt, sugar, turmeric, cilantro, cumin, and 4 tablespoons of the coconut milk. Mix thoroughly, using clean hands to knead the spices into the meat. Cover and leave to marinate for at least 2 hours.

PREPARATION: 5 MINUTES +
2 HOURS MARINATING
COOKING: 45 MINUTES
SERVES: 4

SPRING ROLLS

Poh piah tod

1 Make the filling: heat the oil in a wok or large deep skillet. Add the garlic mixture and stir-fry for 1 minute until golden brown. Add the crabmeat, shrimp, and pork, and stir-fry for 10–12 minutes, or until lightly cooked. Add the vermicelli, mushrooms, *nam pla*, soy sauce, sugar, and scallions and stir-fry for 5 minutes, until all the liquid has been absorbed. Set aside to cool.

3 Fold the sides over the filling and then roll up like a sausage. Brush the top edge with more beaten egg and then seal. Keep the filled rolls covered while you make the remaining spring rolls in the same way.

2 Separate the spring roll wrappers and spread them out under a clean tea towel to keep them soft. Put about 2 tablespoons of the filling on each spring roll wrapper, and brush the left and right borders with beaten egg.

1 x ½ pound package spring roll wrappers, each 5 inches square
1 egg, beaten
oil for deep-frying
For the filling:
2 tablespoons vegetable oil
2 tablespoons garlic mixture (see page 110)
¼ pound crabmeat
¼ pound uncooked shrimp, shelled and finely chopped
¼ pound ground pork
¼ pound vermicelli, soaked in boiling water until soft and cut into ½-inch lengths
1 cup chopped mushrooms
2 tablespoons *nam pla* (fish sauce)
2 tablespoons light soy sauce
1 teaspoon sugar
5 scallions, finely chopped

4 Heat the oil in a wok or deep-fat fryer and cook the spring rolls, a few at a time, for 5–8 minutes, or until golden brown. Turn them once during cooking so that they brown evenly. Drain them on absorbent paper towels and serve them hot.

PREPARATION: 25 MINUTES
COOKING: 5–8 MINUTES
SERVES: 6

THAI DUMPLINGS

Kah nom jeeb

1 Put the pork, crabmeat, egg, water chestnuts, garlic mixture, *nam pla*, soy sauce, and cornstarch in a food processor or blender and process until well mixed, but not puréed. Alternatively, you can knead the ingredients by hand.

2 Trim 1/2 inch off the 4 corners of each wonton wrapper to make an octagonal shape. Place a teaspoon of the pork filling mixture in the center of each wrapper.

PREPARATION: 25 MINUTES
COOKING: 15 MINUTES
SERVES: 8–10

3 Bring up all the edges into the center to make a cup shape. Pinch the sides of the wonton "cup" between your forefinger and thumb to form pleats. Shell the shrimp, remove the veins, and cut in half lengthwise. Tuck half a shrimp into each wonton dumpling.

1/2 pound ground pork
1/2 pound crabmeat
1 egg
1/4 pound canned water chestnuts, drained
1 tablespoon garlic mixture (see page 110)
1 tablespoon *nam pla* (fish sauce)
1 tablespoon soy sauce
1 tablespoon cornstarch
40 wonton wrappers (ones that are suitable for steaming)
20 uncooked shrimp
oil for deep-frying
To serve:
4 tablespoons soy sauce
4 tablespoons sweet and sour sauce
1 tablespoon garlic oil (see page 111)

4 Arrange the filled wontons in the top of one or two greased steamers and then steam gently for 15 minutes. Meanwhile, prepare the dipping sauce: mix the soy sauce and sweet and sour sauce together in a small bowl. Serve the hot dumplings, sprinkled with garlic oil, with the dipping sauce or some chile sauce.

CHICKEN DUMPLINGS

Kha nom jeeb sai gai

3 tablespoons glutinous rice flour

2¼ cups rice flour

3 tablespoons arrowroot

1½ cups water

2½ tablespoons vegetable oil

For the filling:

4 tablespoons vegetable oil

2 tablespoons garlic mixture (see page 110)

1 pound ground chicken

1 onion, finely chopped

3 tablespoons *nam pla* (fish sauce)

3 tablespoons sugar

To serve:

2 tablespoons garlic oil (see page 111)

½ cucumber, sliced

5 scallions, sliced

2 Transfer the mixture to a large bowl and allow to cool slightly. When it is just warm, add the remaining arrowroot and knead the dough until it is smooth and shiny. Cover the bowl with a damp cloth while you make the filling.

3 Make the filling: heat 2 tablespoons of the oil in a wok and stir-fry the garlic mixture for 1 minute. Add the chicken and stir-fry for 4–5 minutes, until cooked. Stir in the onion, *nam pla*, and sugar, and stir-fry until the liquid is absorbed. Transfer to a bowl and leave to cool.

1 Make the dough: put both the rice flours in a saucepan with 1 tablespoon of the arrowroot, and stir in the water and vegetable oil. Cook over a moderate heat, stirring constantly, until the mixture forms a ball and leaves the sides of the pan clean.

PREPARATION: 30 MINUTES
COOKING: 10–15 MINUTES
SERVES: 6

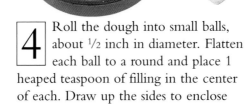

4 Roll the dough into small balls, about ½ inch in diameter. Flatten each ball to a round and place 1 heaped teaspoon of filling in the center of each. Draw up the sides to enclose the filling or fold over to form semi-circles, and crimp the edges. Line the top of a steamer with oiled foil or banana leaves, and arrange the dumplings on top. Steam over boiling water for 10–15 minutes. Serve brushed with garlic oil and garnished with sliced cucumber and sliced scallions.

FRIED GOLDEN BAGS

Tang tong

20 wonton wrappers
20 fresh chives, approx. 4 inches long
oil for deep-frying

For the crabmeat filling:

3 ounces canned water chestnuts, chopped
¹/₂ pound crabmeat
2 ounces uncooked shrimp, shelled and chopped
2 teaspoons garlic mixture (see page 110)
2 scallions, chopped
1 fresh green chile, seeded and chopped
1 tablespoon dark soy sauce
1 tablespoon *nam pla* (fish sauce)

To serve:

plum sauce or chile sauce (see page 110)

1 Make the filling: put all the filling ingredients in a large mixing bowl and mix together until thoroughly combined. You should end up with a thick paste.

PREPARATION: 25 MINUTES
COOKING: 5–10 MINUTES
SERVES: 4–5

2 Spread the wonton wrappers out on a flat surface and divide the crabmeat filling equally between them, putting a spoonful in the center of each wrapper. Pull the 4 corners up into the middle to make little bags.

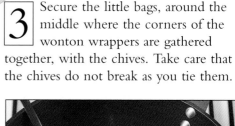

3 Secure the little bags, around the middle where the corners of the wonton wrappers are gathered together, with the chives. Take care that the chives do not break as you tie them.

4 Heat the oil for deep-frying in a wok or deep-fryer. Fry the little bags in batches, a few at a time, until they are crisp and golden brown. Remove and drain on absorbent paper towels. Serve very hot with either plum sauce or chile sauce.

FRIED HOT FISH BALLS

Tod mun pla

1 Put the garlic, black peppercorns, cilantro, sugar, and dried red chiles in a food processor or blender and work to a smooth paste.

2 Add the fish fillets, a little at a time, and continue working to a smooth paste. Add the flour and soy sauce and process for a few seconds. Transfer the mixture to a bowl.

PREPARATION: 15 MINUTES
COOKING: 5–10 MINUTES
SERVES: 4

3 Shape the mixture into 20 small balls, about 1 inch in diameter. Heat the oil in a wok or deep frying pan and then fry the fish balls, a few at a time, until golden brown all over. Remove with a slotted spoon, drain and keep warm.

4 garlic cloves, minced
20 black peppercorns
4 stems cilantro, finely chopped
pinch of sugar
3 large dried red chiles
1½ pounds fish fillets, skinned
1 tablespoon all-purpose flour
1 tablespoon soy sauce
5 tablespoons vegetable oil
For the salad:
½ cucumber, peeled and thinly sliced
1 teaspoon distilled vinegar
2 tablespoons water
1 teaspoon sugar
2 scallions, finely chopped
1 small carrot, peeled and grated

4 Arrange the cucumber slices in a serving dish. Mix together the vinegar, water, sugar, scallions, and carrot, and sprinkle over the cucumber. Serve the cucumber salad with the fried hot fish balls.

SHRIMP CURRY

Kaeng keao wan kung

1 Put the coconut milk in a jug and chill in the refrigerator for at least 1 hour, or until the thick cream rises to the surface. Scoop 1 cup off the top and put into a wok or heavy saucepan. Reserve the remaining coconut milk for later.

3 Shell and devein the shrimp and wash them under running water. Pat dry and add to the mixture in the wok. Stir-fry for 3–4 minutes, until they are firm and pink.

2 Bring the coconut milk to a boil and then simmer, uncovered, stirring occasionally, until the coconut oil begins to bubble to the surface and the liquid reduces to a quarter of its original volume. Add the curry paste and *laos* and bring to a boil. Cook over a medium to high heat until most of the liquid evaporates.

| 3 cups coconut milk (see page 111) |
| 2 tablespoons green curry paste (see page 111) |
| 2 teaspoons ground *laos* |
| 1½ pounds uncooked shrimp |
| 2 tablespoons nam pla (fish sauce) |
| 1 tablespoon fresh green chile, cut into 1-inch strips |
| 4 fresh basil leaves |

4 Stir in the remaining coconut milk and *nam pla* and simmer for 6–8 minutes, stirring occasionally. Serve garnished with strips of green chile and basil leaves.

PREPARATION: 10 MINUTES + 1 HOUR CHILLING
COOKING: 30–35 MINUTES
SERVES: 4–6

CRAB IN THE SHELL

Bhou jah

4 crab shells, washed and dried

a few fresh cilantro leaves

2 fresh red chiles,
seeded and cut into strips

2 eggs

oil for deep-frying

chile sauce or *nam pla* (fish sauce) to serve

For the filling:

3 ounces crabmeat

3 ounces minced uncooked shrimp

½ pounds ground pork

1 egg

1 tablespoon garlic mixture (see page 110)

1 tablespoon *nam pla* (fish sauce)

1 tablespoon soy sauce

2 Pack the filling mixture into the crab shells and place them in the top of a steamer. Scatter with cilantro leaves and strips of red chile. Steam the filled crab shells over boiling water for 15 minutes, and then set aside to cool.

1 Prepare the filling: mix the crabmeat, shrimp, and pork in a small bowl. Stir in the egg, garlic mixture, *nam pla*, and soy sauce, and mix well together.

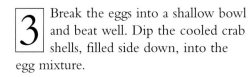

3 Break the eggs into a shallow bowl and beat well. Dip the cooled crab shells, filled side down, into the egg mixture.

4 Heat the oil in a wok or deep-fat fryer, and fry the filled crab shells, one at a time, for 1–2 minutes, or until the egg coating is golden. Remove with a slotted spoon and then drain on absorbent paper towels. Serve the crabs with chile sauce or *nam pla*.

PREPARATION: 30 MINUTES
COOKING: 4–8 MINUTES
SERVES: 4

SOUR FISH CURRY

Kang som pla

1½ cups water
1 pound white fish fillet, sliced
2 tablespoons *nam pla* (fish sauce)
1 tablespoon sugar
2 tablespoons lemon juice
¾ pound mixed vegetables, e.g. shredded cabbage, sliced zucchini, trimmed green beans and broccoli florets
For the kang som paste:
6 fresh or dried red chiles, seeded and sliced
2 teaspoons salt
1 tablespoon chopped mild onion
2 teaspoons shrimp paste

2 Bring the measured water to a boil in a medium-sized saucepan. Add half of the sliced fish fillet, then lower the heat and simmer gently for 5 minutes. Remove the fish with a slotted spoon.

3 Put the cooked fish in a food processor or blender together with the kang som paste. Blend the fish and paste until thick and smooth. Alternatively, pound the fish mixture in a mortar with a pestle.

1 Make the kang som paste: if using dried chiles, soak them in cold water for 10 minutes and then squeeze out as much liquid as possible. Put the chiles in a mortar with the salt and pound to a paste. Add the onion and shrimp paste and grind until smooth.

4 Transfer the puréed mixture to a clean saucepan and bring slowly to the boil. Stir in the *nam pla*, sugar, and lemon juice. Add the vegetables and the remaining fish and stir well. Cover the pan and simmer for 10 minutes. Serve immediately.

PREPARATION: 20 MINUTES
COOKING: 25 MINUTES
SERVES: 4

SEAFOOD IN BATTER

Gung pla choob pang tod

1 Combine the garlic mixture and *nam pla* in a shallow bowl. Shell and devein the shrimp and cut the squid into rings (if using). Add to the dish and turn gently in the garlic marinade. Set aside for 5 minutes.

3 Remove the shrimp and squid from the garlic marinade and dip them quickly into the prepared tempura batter. Set aside while you heat the oil ready for frying.

2 teaspoons garlic mixture (see page 110)
2 teaspoons *nam pla* (fish sauce)
1 pound mixed seafood, e.g. shrimp and squid
oil for deep-frying
For the tempura batter:
1 egg
²/₃ cup cold water
1 cup all-purpose flour
2 tablespoons cornstarch
1 teaspoon baking soda
To serve:
shrimp dipping sauce (see page 110)

PREPARATION: 25 MINUTES
COOKING: 5–10 MINUTES
SERVES: 4

2 Make the tempura batter: lightly beat together the egg and water in a small bowl. Stir in the flour, cornstarch, and the baking soda. Do not over-mix; the batter should have a slightly lumpy texture.

4 Heat the oil for deep-frying in a deep wok, a skillet, or a deep-fat fryer. When it is hot, fry the battered seafood, a few at a time, until puffed up and golden. Remove with a slotted spoon and drain on absorbent paper towels. Serve immediately with shrimp dipping sauce.

MUSSELS WITH THAI HERBS

Hoy mangpoo ob mor din

10 cups fresh mussels in their shells

5 cups water

6 kaffir lime leaves

peel of 1 lemon

2 stalks lemon grass

1 tablespoon salt

3 fresh red chiles, sliced

3 scallions, chopped

a few cilantro leaves, torn

2 Put the water in a large saucepan and bring to the boil. Add the kaffir lime leaves, lemon peel, lemon grass, and salt. Add the mussels, cover the pan and bring back to a boil.

1 Wash the mussels under running cold water and then clean them thoroughly with a sharp knife. Discard any mussels that are open.

3 Cook the mussels, shaking the pan occasionally, until the mussels open. Drain them, reserving half of the cooking liquor. Transfer the mussels to a deep serving dish, discarding any that have not opened.

4 Strain the reserved stock, discarding the lime leaves, lemon peel, and lemon grass. Bring to the boil, add the sliced red chiles and scallions, and then boil vigorously for 2 minutes. Pour over the mussels and serve sprinkled with cilantro.

PREPARATION: 20 MINUTES
COOKING: 20 MINUTES
SERVES: 4

SHRIMP IN COCONUT SAUCE

Gung penang

16 uncooked jumbo shrimp
2 tablespoons oil
1 large onion, finely chopped
2 stalks lemon grass, chopped
2 fresh red chiles, sliced
1-inch piece fresh root ginger, shredded
1 tablespoon ground cumin
1 tablespoon ground cilantro
2 tablespoons *nam pla* (fish sauce)
1 cup thick coconut milk (see page 111)
3 tablespoons roasted peanuts, coarsely ground
2 tomatoes, skinned and chopped
1 teaspoon sugar
juice of ½ lime
fresh cilantro leaves, chopped

2 Heat the oil in a wok or heavy skillet. Add the onion and fry until soft and golden. Add the chopped lemon grass, sliced red chiles, ginger, cumin, and cilantro, and sauté for 2 minutes.

3 Add the *nam pla* and coconut milk to the wok. Stir well and then add the peanuts and chopped tomatoes. Cook gently over low heat until the tomato is soft and the flavors of the sauce are well developed.

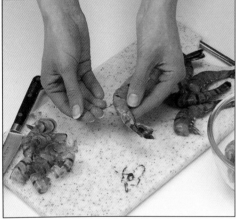

1 Remove the shrimp from their shells, leaving the tails intact. Remove the dark veins running along the back of the shrimp and then slit them down the underside all the way from head to tail.

4 Stir in the prepared shrimp and simmer gently for 5 minutes, or until the shrimp are pink and tender. Add the sugar and transfer to a serving dish. Serve hot sprinkled with lime juice and chopped cilantro leaves.

PREPARATION: 20 MINUTES
COOKING: 17–20 MINUTES
SERVES: 4

STEAMED FISH

Pla pah sah

1 large or 2 medium whole mullet, striped bass or grouper, scaled and cleaned

3 fresh red chiles, seeded and chopped

1/2-inch piece fresh root ginger, grated

3 scallions, chopped

2 garlic cloves, minced

1 stalk lemon grass, chopped

2 tablespoons *nam pla* (fish sauce)

For the stock:

1/4 cup shredded cabbage

2 sticks celery, sliced

1 garlic clove, minced

juice of 1 lime

1 cup fish stock or water

To serve:

chile sauce (see page 110)

2 In a bowl, mix together the chopped red chiles, ginger, scallions, garlic, lemon grass, and *nam pla*. Spread this mixture over the fish.

1 Wash the fish under running cold water, inside and out. Pat dry with absorbent paper towels, and then slash the skin of the fish a few times with a sharp knife.

PREPARATION: 15 MINUTES
COOKING: 25 MINUTES
SERVES: 4

3 Place the fish on a rack or a perforated tray, and set above some boiling water in a large wok. Cover with the lid and steam for 15 minutes. Alternatively, use a large steamer or fish poacher.

4 Combine the cabbage, celery, garlic, lime juice, and fish stock in a saucepan. Bring to a boil, and then pour over the fish in the wok. Continue steaming for 10 minutes, or until the fish is cooked and tender. Serve the steamed fish with the chile sauce.

SPICY FISHCAKES

Tod mun pla

1 Put the chunks of fish fillet and red curry paste in a food processor or blender. Process until the fish is pounded to a paste. Alternatively, pound in a mortar with a pestle.

2 Transfer the fish mixture to a bowl and add the egg, *nam pla*, and sufficient flour to knead with your hands into a stiff mixture. Work in the beans and lime leaves with your hands.

PREPARATION: 20 MINUTES
COOKING: 8–10 MINUTES
SERVES: 4–5

3 Form the fish mixture into 16–20 balls, and, using your hands, flatten each ball into a round, about 1/2 inch thick.

1 pound white fish fillet, skinned and cut into chunks
3 tablespoons red curry paste (see page 111)
1 egg
3 tablespoons *nam pla* (fish sauce)
1–2 tablespoons rice flour
3 ounces thin green beans, finely chopped
1 tablespoon finely shredded kaffir lime leaves
oil for deep-frying
To serve:
chile sauce (see page 110)

4 Heat the oil in a wok or large deep skillet, and fry the fishcakes, a few at a time, for 4–5 minutes on each side, until they are cooked and golden. Take care not to overcook them. Drain on absorbent paper towels and then serve hot with chile sauce and a cucumber salad, if wished.

BEEF WITH CASHEW NUTS

Nauh bhud med ma maung

1 Heat ½ tablespoon of the sesame oil in a small skillet, and fry the dried red chiles until crisp. Drain on absorbent paper towels to absorb the oil, and set aside while you stir-fry the beef and vegetables.

| 3 tablespoons sesame oil |
| ½ tablespoon chopped dried red chiles |
| 1 garlic clove, finely chopped |
| 1 onion, sliced |
| 1-inch piece fresh root ginger, chopped |
| 2–3 kaffir lime leaves, torn |
| 1 pound lean beef, e.g. prime steak, cut into strips |
| freshly ground black pepper |
| 1 tablespoon soy sauce |
| 1 teaspoon sugar |
| 1 sweet red pepper, seeded and sliced |
| 1 sweet green pepper, seeded and sliced |
| 4 scallions, sliced diagonally |
| 1 cup roasted cashew nuts |

3 Add the kaffir lime leaves and strips of beef, and stir-fry for 2–3 minutes. Season to taste with black pepper, and stir the soy sauce and sugar into the beef mixture.

4 Add the sweet peppers and scallions and stir-fry for 2–3 minutes. Add the reserved fried chiles and the roasted cashew nuts and quickly stir them through the mixture. Serve immediately with some boiled rice or fried noodles.

2 Heat the remaining sesame oil in a wok or a large skillet. Add the garlic, onion, and ginger and stir-fry quickly for about 3 minutes over high heat, until the onion is soft and golden-brown.

PREPARATION: 10 MINUTES
COOKING: 10 MINUTES
SERVES: 4

SWEET AND SOUR PORK

Bhud priew wharn

2 tablespoons vegetable oil

1 garlic clove, minced

1 pound pork tenderloin

1/4 teaspoon freshly ground black pepper

1 tablespoon *nam pla* (fish sauce)

1 teaspoon sugar

1/2 cucumber

3 scallions

1 tomato

1 fresh or canned pineapple ring, chopped

4 tablespoons chicken or vegetable stock

1 Heat the oil in a wok or deep skillet. Add the minced garlic and stir-fry quickly until it is golden, but not browned.

2 Slice the pork thinly and add to the wok, together with the freshly ground black pepper, *nam pla*, and sugar. Stir-fry for 6–8 minutes, until the pork is cooked.

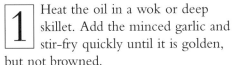

4 Add the vegetables to the wok with the chopped pineapple and the chicken or vegetable stock. Stir-fry for 3 minutes. Serve hot with plain boiled rice or noodles.

3 Prepare the vegetables: shred the cucumber and slice the scallions across diagonally. Skin the tomato by plunging it into boiling water, and then coarsely chop it.

PREPARATION: 10 MINUTES
COOKING: 11–13 MINUTES
SERVES: 4

SLICED PORK WITH HOT SAUCES

Moo thod katiem prik

3/4 pound pork tenderloin
1/2 teaspoon salt
1/4 teaspoon white pepper
2 tablespoons butter and oil, mixed
3 garlic cloves
1/2-inch piece fresh root ginger, chopped
2 fresh red chiles, chopped
1 1/2 teaspoons ground cumin
For the chile and ginger sauce:
2 fresh red chiles
1-inch piece fresh root ginger, peeled
1/2 onion, grated
salt
For the tomato and chile sauce:
2 tomatoes, skinned and chopped
2 garlic cloves, minced
salt
pinch of sugar
1 teaspoon hot chile powder

1 Slice the pork thinly, and rub with salt and pepper. Heat the butter and oil in a wok or small skillet over a moderate heat. Add the pork and stir-fry until lightly browned. Remove from the wok and keep warm.

3 Make the chile and ginger sauce: put the chiles, ginger, onion, and salt in a pestle and mortar. Pound the ingredients to a smooth, thick paste.

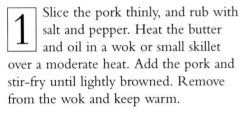

2 Chop the garlic finely and add to the wok with the ginger, chiles, and cumin. Stir-fry for 2 minutes, and then return the pork to the wok. Stir-fry for 2 minutes over a low heat, or until the meat is tender. If necessary, add a sprinkling of water to keep the meat moist.

4 Make the tomato and chile sauce: put the chopped tomatoes and garlic in a small bowl, and mix in the salt, a good pinch of sugar, and the hot chile powder. Serve the stir-fried pork with the two hot sauces.

PREPARATION: 15 MINUTES
COOKING: 8–10 MINUTES
SERVES: 4

STUFFED THAI CREPE

Kai yud sai

3 tablespoons vegetable oil

1 garlic clove, minced

1/4 pound ground pork

freshly ground black pepper

1 tablespoon *nam pla* (fish sauce)

1/2 tablespoon sugar

2/3 cup finely chopped onion

1 tomato, skinned and chopped

3 eggs, beaten

To garnish:

fresh cilantro leaves

2 Stir-fry the pork and vegetable mixture in the wok for 5–10 minutes, until the pork is cooked and lightly browned, and the onion is tender and golden.

3 Heat the remaining oil in a clean wok or omelet pan, tilting it so that the oil coats the entire surface of the wok or pan. Pour away and discard any excess oil. Pour in the beaten eggs and swirl around the inside of the wok to form a thin skin.

1 Heat 2 tablespoons of the oil in a small wok or skillet. Add the garlic and stir-fry quickly until golden-brown. Add the ground pork, black pepper, *nam pla*, sugar, chopped onion, and tomato.

4 Put the stir-fried vegetable and pork mixture in the center of the omelet. Fold down the 4 sides to make a neat parcel. Slide out on to a warm serving dish, folded-side down, and serve garnished with cilantro leaves.

PREPARATION: 10 MINUTES
COOKING: 12–17 MINUTES
SERVES: 2

MASAMAN CURRY

Kang masaman

2 pounds lean beef

5 cups water

7 ounces creamed coconut,
roughly chopped

1¼ cups roasted peanuts

nam pla (fish sauce), to taste

3 tablespoons tamarind water (see page 111)

coconut sugar to taste

For the curry paste:

1 teaspoon oil

7 dried chiles, seeded and finely chopped

½ teaspoon freshly ground black pepper

2 tablespoons cilantro seeds

2 tablespoons cumin seeds

1 tablespoon shredded lemon grass

1 cinnamon stalk

5 cardamom seeds

¼ whole nutmeg, grated

1 teaspoon salt

1 onion, very finely minced

5 garlic cloves, minced

½ teaspoon dried shrimp paste

2 Make the curry paste: heat the oil in a pan and add the chiles, black pepper, cilantro, cumin, lemon grass, cinnamon, cardamom, and nutmeg. Cook over low heat, stirring constantly, until the mixture browns.

3 Transfer to a mortar or an electric blender or food processor, and work to a smooth paste. Add the salt, chopped onion, garlic, and dried shrimp paste, and continue working the mixture until smooth.

4 Remove the cooked meat from the pan and keep warm. Add the creamed coconut to the liquid in the pan and heat gently, stirring. Add the peanuts and *nam pla*. Boil hard until the liquid is reduced by one-third. Add the curry paste and simmer for 5 minutes, stirring. Return the meat to the pan, cover and bring to a boil. Cook over a medium heat for a few minutes. Add the tamarind water and coconut sugar. Serve hot.

1 Cut the beef into 1-inch squares, trimming off any excess fat. Put the beef and water in a large saucepan and bring to a boil. Lower the heat, cover the pan and then simmer for about 1 hour, or until the meat is tender.

PREPARATION: 15 MINUTES
COOKING: 1½ HOURS
SERVES: 6

BEEF IN OYSTER SAUCE

Nauh bhud num mun hoi hed

1 Put the oyster sauce, cornstarch, and freshly ground black pepper in a small shallow dish, and mix well together until the mixture is well blended and smooth.

2 Cut the prime steak into thin slices. Add to the oyster sauce mixture and mix in gently until well coated. Set aside to marinate for at least 15 minutes before cooking.

3 Heat the oil in a wok or deep skillet. Add the minced garlic and stir-fry until golden. Add the marinated steak and continue stir-frying for 3–4 minutes, until the meat is browned and medium-cooked.

| 2 tablespoons oyster sauce |
| 2 teaspoons cornstarch |
| $^{1}/_{2}$ teaspoon freshly ground black pepper |
| $^{1}/_{2}$ pound prime steak |
| 2 tablespoons vegetable oil |
| 1 garlic clove, minced |
| $^{1}/_{4}$ pound mushrooms, sliced |
| 6 scallions, sliced diagonally |
| $^{1}/_{2}$ cup chicken stock or water |

4 Add the sliced mushrooms, scallions and the chicken stock. Stir well and then cook gently for 2 minutes. Transfer to a serving dish and serve with plain boiled rice or some fried noodles.

PREPARATION: 10 MINUTES +
15 MINUTES MARINATING
COOKING: 7–8 MINUTES
SERVES: 4

THICK RED BEEF CURRY

Kang panag nua

3/4 pound beef brisket, thinly sliced

1 tablespoon vegetable oil

2 tablespoons red curry paste (see page 111)

3/4 cup coconut milk (see page 111)

1 tablespoon *nam pla* (fish sauce)

1 tablespoon sugar

4 kaffir lime leaves

1–2 fresh green chiles

2 sprigs fresh basil

2 Heat the oil in a saucepan over moderate heat. Add the prepared red curry paste and stir-fry for 1 minute. Stir in 2 tablespoons of the coconut milk and cook, stirring constantly, for 5 minutes.

3 Add the cooked beef slices to the saucepan together with the *nam pla*, sugar, the remaining coconut milk and lime leaves. Bring to a boil, then lower the heat and simmer, stirring occasionally, for 15 minutes.

1 Place the beef in a medium-sized saucepan. Add sufficient water to cover and bring to a boil. Lower the heat and simmer for 1-1¼ hours, or until the meat is tender, skimming the liquid occasionally. Remove the beef slices with a slotted spoon and set aside.

4 Wearing gloves if possible, slice the chiles into thin rounds and remove the seeds. Just before serving the curry, stir in the sliced chiles and the sprigs of basil.

PREPARATION: 5 MINUTES
COOKING: 1¼-1½ HOURS
SERVES: 2–3

FRIED PORK BALLS

Moo tod

1 Put the cilantro stems, freshly ground black pepper, garlic, and sugar in a mortar or blender, and then work to a smooth paste.

2 Put the pork and the cilantro paste in a food processor or blender and add the *nam pla*. Process until the mixture is thick and smooth, and transfer to a bowl.

3 Form the mixture into about 20 small balls, approximately 1 inch in diameter. Roll the pork balls lightly in some flour.

2 teaspoons chopped fresh cilantro stems
2 teaspoons freshly ground black pepper
4 garlic cloves, peeled
pinch of sugar
1 pound ground pork
2 tablespoons *nam pla* (fish sauce)
flour for coating
4–5 tablespoons vegetable oil
To garnish:
fresh cilantro leaves

PREPARATION: 15 MINUTES
COOKING: 12 MINUTES
SERVES: 4

4 Heat the oil in a wok or deep skillet and add about 5 pork balls. Fry over moderate heat for 2–3 minutes, or until no liquid is released from the balls when they are pierced with a knife. Remove from the wok and keep warm while you fry the remaining balls in the same way. Serve hot, garnished with fresh cilantro leaves.

CHICKEN CURRY

Kaeng phet kai

5 ounces creamed coconut, roughly chopped

²/₃ cup water

4 large chicken breasts, boned, skinned and sliced

1 eggplant, peeled, cubed and blanched

1-inch piece fresh root ginger, chopped

a few kaffir lime leaves, torn

For the curry paste:

½ teaspoon roasted cilantro seeds

1 stalk lemon grass, finely chopped

grated peel of 1 lime

2 fresh green chiles, seeded and chopped

1 teaspoon cumin seeds

1 teaspoon shrimp paste

3 garlic cloves, minced

1 small onion, finely chopped

To serve:

some fresh basil leaves

2 fresh green chiles, chopped

3 Add the curry paste to the reserved coconut liquid and heat gently, stirring continuously. Continue stirring over a low heat until the liquid starts to evaporate and thicken.

1 Put the creamed coconut and water in a large saucepan and heat gently, stirring all the time, until the coconut melts. Add the chicken and simmer for 10 minutes. Remove the chicken and keep warm. Reserve the coconut liquid.

PREPARATION: 10 MINUTES
COOKING: 30 MINUTES
SERVES: 4

2 Make the curry paste: grind all the ingredients together in a mortar with a pestle until you have a smooth paste. Alternatively, blend them at high speed in a food processor or blender until smooth.

4 Add the reserved chicken, cubed eggplant, ginger, and kaffir lime leaves, and cook gently for a few minutes. Serve the curry sprinkled with basil leaves and green chiles, with some noodles or boiled rice.

STUFFED CHICKEN WINGS

Peag gai sord sai

1 Prepare the chicken: remove the top part of each wing. Your aim is to bone the wings without damaging the skin. Cut around the bones with a small sharp knife and ease them out. Alternatively, break the wing joint and work the bones loose with your fingers. Turn the wings inside out to remove the bones.

2 Make the filling: put the chicken and vermicelli in a bowl with the chopped water chestnuts, garlic mixture, beaten egg, nam pla, and soy sauce. Mix until the ingredients are thoroughly combined.

PREPARATION: 30 MINUTES
COOKING: 23–24 MINUTES
SERVES: 4

3 Carefully stuff each boned chicken wing with the stuffing mixture. Place them in the top of 1 large or 2 small steamers, and steam over boiling water for 20 minutes. Remove and cool.

16 chicken wings
³/₄ pound ground chicken
¹/₄ pound vermicelli, softened in boiling water and cut in ¹/₂-inch lengths
¹/₄ pound drained canned water chestnuts, finely chopped
1 tablespoon garlic mixture (see page 110)
1 egg, lightly beaten
2 tablespoons *nam pla* (fish sauce)
2 tablespoons soy sauce
For stir-frying:
1 tablespoon oil
2 tablespoons garlic mixture (see page 110)
2 tablespoons *nam pla* (fish sauce)
chile sauce to serve (see page 110)

4 Heat the oil for stir-frying in a wok or large skillet. Add the garlic mixture and *nam pla*, and then add the chicken wings. Stir-fry briskly for 3–4 minutes, until golden. Serve the chicken with some chile sauce.

GINGER CHICKEN WITH HONEY

Pad king kai

5 scallions

2-ounce piece fresh root ginger

2 tablespoons vegetable oil

3 chicken breasts, skinned and boned

3 chicken livers, chopped

1 onion, sliced

3 garlic cloves, minced

2 tablespoons dried Chinese black mushrooms,
soaked in warm water for 20 minutes

2 tablespoons soy sauce

1 tablespoon honey

2 Heat the oil in a wok or a large heavy-based skillet. Cut the chicken into small pieces and add to the wok with the chicken livers. Fry for 5 minutes, then remove with a slotted spoon and set aside.

3 Add the onion to the wok and fry gently until soft. Add the garlic and the drained mushrooms and stir-fry for 1 minute. Return the cooked chicken pieces and chicken livers to the wok.

1 Cut the scallions into 1/2-inch pieces. Put in a bowl, cover with cold water and leave to soak until required. Chop the ginger finely, mix with a little cold water, then drain and squeeze to remove its hotness. Rinse under cold running water and drain.

4 Mix the soy sauce and honey, stirring until blended. Pour over the chicken and stir well. Add the drained ginger and stir-fry for 2–3 minutes. Add the drained scallions, and transfer to a serving dish. This dish tastes even better if it is cooked the day before and then reheated.

PREPARATION: 15 MINUTES
COOKING: 15 MINUTES
SERVES: 4

RICE VERMICELLI WITH SAUCE

Pad mee krob

1 Heat the oil for deep-frying in a heavy saucepan or deep-fat fryer to 375°. Fry the rice vermicelli in small batches for about 30 seconds, until the strands swell and float. Drain and set aside. Take care that you fry only a little at a time as it expands a lot and could overflow the pan.

3 Now add the shelled shrimp and crabmeat and cook for 2–3 minutes, until the shrimp firm up and turn pink. Stir in the brown sugar, tamarind water, salt, and soy sauce.

2 Make the sauce: heat the oil in a wok or deep skillet. Add the onion and garlic and fry for a few minutes, until lightly brown.

vegetable oil for deep-frying
2 ounces rice vermicelli, broken into pieces
For the sauce:
1 tablespoon vegetable oil
1 onion, finely chopped
2 garlic cloves, minced
½ pound uncooked shrimp, shelled
3 ounces crabmeat
2 teaspoons brown sugar
2 tablespoons tamarind water (see page 111)
1 teaspoon salt
1 tablespoon soy sauce
To garnish:
2 teaspoons finely grated orange peel
2 red chiles, shredded
chopped cilantro leaves
¼ pound fresh bean sprouts

4 Add the fried vermicelli and stir well. Adjust the seasoning if necessary, and then heat through gently. Transfer to a warm serving dish and garnish with orange peel, chiles, and cilantro. Arrange the bean sprouts around the edge of the dish. Serve hot.

PREPARATION: 15 MINUTES
COOKING: 10 MINUTES
SERVES: 4

RICE VERMICELLI IN COCONUT MILK

Meeh ka ti

3 In a large wok or saucepan, bring the coconut milk to a boil. Cook over a high heat for 10 minutes, until a film of oil forms on top. Stir in the onion, shrimp, soy bean flavoring, sugar, and tamarind or lemon juice. Cook for 5 minutes, and then transfer half of the mixture to a bowl and keep warm.

1 Bring a large saucepan of water to a boil, then add the soaked rice vermicelli and cook, stirring occasionally, for 15 minutes. Drain the vermicelli well and set aside.

2 Heat the oil in an omelet pan or small skillet and add the eggs. Tilt the pan to form an omelet, lifting the sides of the omelet to allow any uncooked egg mixture to flow underneath. Remove the cooked, set omelet from the pan and slice into thin shreds. Keep warm.

PREPARATION: 15 MINUTES +
SOAKING TIME
COOKING: 45 MINUTES
SERVES: 4

½ pound soaked rice vermicelli
2 teaspoons oil
2 eggs, beaten
2 cups coconut milk (see page 111)
½ onion, roughly chopped
½ pound uncooked shrimp, shelled
4 tablespoons salted soy bean flavoring
2 tablespoons sugar
2 tablespoons tamarind juice or 1 tablespoon lemon juice
¾ pound bean sprouts
¼ pound scallions, chopped
To garnish:
3 tablespoons chopped cilantro leaves
2 red chiles, seeded and sliced
1 lemon, sliced lengthways

4 Add the reserved vermicelli to the mixture in the wok. Mix well and cook for 5 minutes. Stir in half of the bean sprouts and scallions. Pile the vermicelli mixture on to a serving dish and top with the reserved shrimp mixture and shredded omelet. Garnish the dish with cilantro, chiles, and lemon slices, and serve hot with the remaining bean sprouts and scallions.

CRISPY RICE WITH DIPPING SAUCE

Khow tung nah tung

1¼ cups glutinous rice

oil for deep-frying

For the sauce:

½ cup coconut milk (see page 111)

¼ cup ground pork

2 ounces minced shrimp

1 teaspoon garlic mixture (see page 110)

1½ tablespoons *nam pla*

1½ tablespoons sugar

¼ cup finely chopped onion

⅓ cup ground roasted peanuts

To garnish:

cilantro leaves

crisply fried strips of red chile

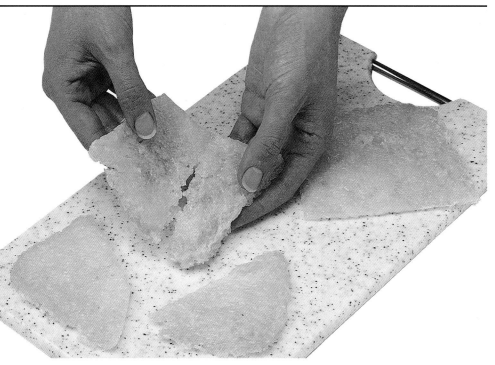

1 Put the rice in a saucepan, cover with water, and boil until the rice is sticky and thoroughly cooked. Drain through a sieve and spread it out in a very thin layer on some greased cookie sheets. Press down well and leave to dry in a warm place or a cool oven at 250°. This drying process takes several hours.

PREPARATION: 20 MINUTES +
DRYING TIME
COOKING: 35 MINUTES
SERVES: 4

2 When completely dry and firm, remove the rice from the cookie sheets with a spatula or fish slice and then break into large pieces.

3 Heat the oil until it is very hot and then drop in some of the rice pieces. Deep-fry quickly until golden. Remove from the oil and drain on absorbent paper towels. Cook the remaining rice in the same way.

4 Bring the coconut milk to a boil in a saucepan. Stir in the pork and shrimp, and add the garlic mixture, *nam pla*, sugar, onion, and peanuts. Mix well, reduce the heat, and simmer for 20 minutes, stirring occasionally. Pour into a serving dish and garnish with cilantro and chile strips. Serve as a dip with the crispy rice.

FRIED RICE WITH PORK

Khow bhud mhoo

1 Crush the garlic in a pestle and mortar, or using a garlic crush. Heat the oil in a wok or a large deep skillet. Add the garlic and stir-fry for 1 minute, until golden-brown.

3 Break the eggs into the wok or skillet, and cook for 2 minutes, stirring vigorously. Add the tomato paste, sugar, the remaining soy sauce, and the sliced onion. Stir-fry briskly for 1 minute.

4 Add the rice and continue stir-frying for 5 minutes. Transfer the mixture to a shallow serving dish or 4 serving plates and garnish with the sliced cucumber, lemon wedges, cilantro leaves, and shredded red chile. Serve immediately.

2 Add the slices of pork tenderloin to the wok together with 1 teaspoon of the light soy sauce and then stir-fry for 5 minutes over medium heat.

1 garlic clove
2 tablespoons vegetable oil
1/4 pound pork tenderloin, sliced
3 tablespoons light soy sauce
2 eggs
1 tablespoon tomato paste
1 tablespoon sugar
1 small onion, sliced
1 1/2 pounds cooked rice (about 1 cup raw weight)
To garnish:
1/4 cucumber, thinly sliced
1 lemon, cut in wedges
2 tablespoons chopped cilantro leaves
1 red chile, seeded and shredded

PREPARATION: 10–15 MINUTES
COOKING: 15 MINUTES
SERVES: 4

THAI-STYLE FRIED RICE STICKS

Geuy teuw bhud Thai

1 Put the rice sticks in a large bowl and cover with cold water. Leave them to soak for at least 2 hours, or until they are soft. Drain the rice sticks well and set aside.

3 Add the dried shrimp, preserved turnip, ground chile, and the crushed peanuts, stirring all the time until well mixed.

2 Heat the oil in a wok or a large deep skillet. Add the garlic and stir-fry for 1 minute, until golden. Add the chicken, crabmeat, and shrimp, and stir-fry for 3 minutes. Stir in the drained rice sticks, *nam pla*, sugar, lemon juice, and pepper, and cook for 1 minute.

PREPARATION: 15 MINUTES +
2 HOURS SOAKING
COOKING: 10 MINUTES
SERVES: 4

¼ pound rice sticks
2 tablespoons vegetable oil
1 garlic clove, minced
¼ pound chicken breast, thinly sliced
¼ pound crabmeat
¼ pound uncooked shrimp, shelled and deveined
2 tablespoons *nam pla* (fish sauce)
2 tablespoons sugar
½ tablespoon lemon juice
¼ teaspoon freshly ground black pepper
1 tablespoon ground dried shrimp
1 tablespoon chopped preserved turnip
½ teaspoon ground chile
2 tablespoons crushed roasted peanuts
1 egg
2 tablespoons chopped scallion tops
¼ pound bean sprouts
To serve:
1 lemon, sliced and quartered
2 ounces fresh bean sprouts

4 Break the egg into the wok and continue stirring. Add the scallion tops and bean sprouts, and then stir-fry for 3 more minutes, until the egg is set and the rice sticks are tender. If the rice sticks are hard, add 2 more tablespoons of water and cook until absorbed. Serve garnished with sliced lemon and bean sprouts.

RICE STICKS WITH BEEF SAUCE

Geuy teuw nah sub

1 Spread out the soaked rice sticks in a large shallow dish. Sprinkle the rice sticks with dark soy sauce and mix thoroughly, using 2 spoons or chopsticks. Make sure that all the rice sticks are coated in soy sauce.

3 Heat the remaining oil in the wok, add the garlic and stir-fry for 1 minute, or until golden-brown. Add the beef, *nam pla*, curry powder, sugar, and black pepper and stir well.

1 pound soaked rice sticks
2 tablespoons dark soy sauce
4 tablespoons vegetable oil
1 garlic clove, minced
1½ cups ground beef
½ tablespoon *nam pla* (fish sauce)
½ tablespoon curry powder
1 teaspoon sugar
¼ teaspoon freshly ground black pepper
1 tablespoon cornstarch
3 tablespoons light soy sauce
1 small onion, chopped
1 tomato, chopped
1½ cups chicken stock
To serve:
1 lettuce, separated into leaves
2 tablespoons chopped cilantro leaves

2 Heat 2 tablespoons of the vegetable oil in a wok or a deep skillet and add the rice sticks. Stir-fry for 3–5 minutes, then transfer to a serving dish and keep warm.

PREPARATION: 10 MINUTES +
2 HOURS SOAKING
COOKING: 25 MINUTES
SERVES: 4–6

4 In a bowl, mix the cornstarch to a paste with the light soy sauce. Stir into the beef mixture and cook for 10–15 minutes, stirring frequently, until the beef is cooked and crumbly. Stir in the onion, tomato, and stock and bring to a boil. Lower the heat and simmer for 5 minutes. Serve the rice sticks on a bed of lettuce topped with the beef mixture. Garnish with cilantro.

SPICY FRIED RICE

Khow bhud khie mau

½ cup ground beef
½ pound canned red kidney beans, drained
1½ tablespoons *nam pla* (fish sauce)
1 tablespoon dark soy sauce
4 red chiles, seeded and finely chopped
3 garlic cloves, minced
½ teaspoon salt
2 tablespoons vegetable oil
10 thin green beans, trimmed and cut in ½-inch lengths
1½ pounds boiled long-grain rice (about 1 cup raw weight)
1 tablespoon sugar
salt and freshly ground black pepper
4 tablespoons roughly chopped fresh basil leaves

1 Put the ground beef and drained kidney beans in a bowl. Mix well and then stir in the *nam pla* and soy sauce. Cover the bowl and set aside for 30 minutes to allow the different flavors to blend.

3 Add the beef and kidney bean mixture to the wok, and cook, stirring constantly, for 3 minutes, or until the beef is lightly browned. Add the green beans and stir-fry for 3 more minutes over a moderate heat.

4 Stir in the cooked rice and sugar, and cook, stirring, until the rice is hot and all the ingredients are thoroughly mixed. Add salt and pepper or more *nam pla* to taste if necessary. Mix in the basil leaves and transfer to a serving dish.

2 Mix the chopped chiles, garlic, and salt together in another bowl. Heat the oil in a wok or large skillet and then add the chile mixture. Stir-fry briskly for 1 minute.

PREPARATION: 10 MINUTES +
30 MINUTES MARINATING
COOKING: 10 MINUTES
SERVES: 4

FRIED NOODLES WITH VEGETABLES

Geuy teuw rard nah

3 Add the shredded cabbage and broccoli florets to the meat mixture in the wok, and stir-fry for 3 more minutes.

1 Heat half of the oil in a wok or large deep skillet. Add half the garlic and stir-fry for 1 minute, until golden-brown. Add the noodles and soy sauce and cook, stirring constantly, for 3–5 minutes. Transfer to a serving dish and keep warm.

4 tablespoons vegetable oil
2 garlic cloves, minced
¼ pound medium-sized egg noodles
2 teaspoons dark soy sauce
¼ pound mixed sliced chicken breast, prepared squid and shelled shrimp
½ teaspoon freshly ground black pepper
2 tablespoons *nam pla* (fish sauce)
¼ pound mixed shredded cabbage and broccoli florets
1¼ cups chicken stock
1 tablespoon cornstarch
1 tablespoon salted soy bean flavoring
2 tablespoons sugar

2 Heat the remaining oil in the wok and add the rest of the garlic. Stir-fry for 1 minute, until golden brown. Add the chicken breast, squid, shrimp, ground black pepper, and *nam pla*. Stir-fry for 5 minutes.

PREPARATION: 10 MINUTES
COOKING: 20 MINUTES
SERVES: 4

4 Stir in the chicken stock. Mix the cornstarch with 2 tablespoons of water and stir into the wok. Add the soy bean flavoring and sugar, and bring to a boil. Lower the heat and cook for 3 minutes, stirring constantly. Pour the thickened sauce over the noodles and serve immediately.

EGG-FRIED NOODLES

Gung ob moh din

4 tablespoons groundnut oil

1 garlic clove, minced

1 small onion, thinly sliced

¼ pound egg noodles

grated peel of 1 lime

2 teaspoons soy sauce

2 tablespoons lime juice

¼ pound sliced chicken breast or pork tenderloin

¼ pound crabmeat or squid

¼ pound shelled shrimp

freshly ground black pepper

1 tablespoon yellow soy bean paste

1 tablespoon *nam pla* (fish sauce)

2 tablespoons brown sugar

2 eggs

2 fresh red chiles, seeded and chopped

a few cilantro leaves, chopped

2 Plunge the egg noodles into boiling water for a few seconds. Drain well and then add to the wok. Stir-fry with the grated lime peel, soy sauce, and lime juice for 3–4 minutes. Remove, drain, and keep warm.

3 Add the remaining oil to the wok together with the chicken, crabmeat, and shrimp. Stir-fry over a high heat until cooked. Season with ground black pepper, and stir in the soy bean paste, *nam pla*, and sugar.

1 Heat half of the oil in a wok or heavy skillet. Add the garlic and the onion, and then stir-fry quickly until golden and tender.

4 Break the eggs into the wok and stir gently until the mixture sets. Add the chiles and check the seasoning. Mix in the noodles and heat through over a low heat. Serve garnished with chopped cilantro.

PREPARATION: 10 MINUTES
COOKING: 20 MINUTES
SERVES: 4

CRISPY RICE VERMICELLI
Meeh grob

oil for deep-frying
5 ounces rice vermicelli
6 tablespoons vegetable oil
1 egg, beaten
1 tablespoon sliced onion
1 tablespoon sliced garlic
2 ounces uncooked shrimp, shelled and cut in half lengthwise
2 ounces chicken breast, thinly sliced
2 tablespoons tamarind water
4 tablespoons brown sugar
1 tablespoon salted soy bean flavoring
1 tablespoon *nam pla* (fish sauce)
To garnish:
1 fresh red chile, seeded and sliced
2 tablespoons chopped cilantro leaves

2 Heat a little of the vegetable oil in a small skillet and add the beaten egg, tilting the pan until it covers the base. Remove the omelet when it is set and cooked, and roll up and cut into thin strips. Keep them warm.

1 Heat the oil in a wok or deep-fat fryer until the temperature reaches 375°. It will be ready when a piece of vermicelli, dropped into the wok, pops open immediately. Deep-fry the vermicelli in batches until it pops and turns a rich creamy color. Remove, drain on absorbent paper towels, and keep warm without covering, or it will become soft.

PREPARATION: 15 MINUTES
COOKING: 17–18 MINUTES
SERVES: 4

3 Heat the remaining oil in a wok and stir-fry the onion and garlic until tender and golden-brown. Remove, drain, and keep warm. Add the shrimp and sliced chicken breast to the wok and stir-fry for 5 minutes. Drain off any excess oil.

4 Stir in the tamarind juice, sugar, soy bean flavoring, and *nam pla*. Cook for 5 minutes until sticky. Add the vermicelli, onion, and garlic to the wok, mix well, and cook over a very low heat for 2–3 minutes. Transfer to a serving dish, top with the omelet strips, and serve garnished with sliced chile and cilantro leaves.

THAI HARD-BOILED EGGS

Khai loog kheoy

1 Bring a saucepan of water to the boil. Stir in the vinegar, then lower the heat and carefully add the eggs. Boil gently for 6–7 minutes, then drain and run the eggs under cold water until cool. Shell them carefully and set aside.

3 Heat the remaining oil in a wok or large skillet. Add the eggs and fry, turning constantly with a wooden spoon, until golden brown. Remove each egg as it browns and drain on absorbent paper towels.

2 Heat ½ tablespoon of the oil in a small wok or skillet. Add the dried red chiles and fry until they are crisp. Drain on absorbent paper towels and set aside.

PREPARATION: 15 MINUTES
COOKING: 15 MINUTES
SERVES: 4–6

1 teaspoon vinegar
6 eggs
4½ tablespoons vegetable oil
1 tablespoon dried red chiles
4 red shallots or 1 small onion, finely chopped
½ cup tamarind sauce
2 teaspoons dark soy sauce

4 Add the shallots to the wok and fry quickly until golden-brown. Transfer to a small dish and keep warm. Pour away all but 2 tablespoons of oil from the wok. Add the tamarind sauce and soy sauce, and boil until the mixture thickens. Meanwhile, quarter the eggs lengthwise and arrange on a serving dish. Pour the tamarind sauce over the top and sprinkle with the fried shallots and chiles.

NORTH-EASTERN BEEF SALAD

Nua nam tok

2 tablespoons glutinous rice

³/₄ pound prime steak

4 tablespoons water

2 onions, finely chopped

3 tablespoons fresh mint leaves, chopped

1 teaspoon ground chile

2 tablespoons lemon juice

2 tablespoons *nam pla* (fish sauce)

¹/₂ teaspoon sugar

For the garnish:

1 lettuce, separated into leaves

2 tablespoons chopped fresh cilantro

2 Put the steak on a rack in a broiler pan and cook under a preheated broiler for about 2 minutes each side. Reduce the heat and cook for 4 minutes. Set aside to cool.

3 Slice the broiled steak thinly and put in a saucepan with the water. Cook over high heat for about 1 minute, stirring constantly.

1 Put the glutinous rice in a saucepan over moderate heat and dry-fry, stirring constantly, for 10 minutes, or until the grains are light brown in color. Remove from the heat and grind in a food processor or pound in a mortar with a pestle until fine.

4 Remove the saucepan from the heat and stir in the ground rice, onions, mint, chile, lemon juice, *nam pla*, and sugar. Arrange the mixture on a bed of lettuce leaves in a shallow serving dish. Scatter the chopped cilantro over the top and serve immediately.

PREPARATION: 20 MINUTES
COOKING: 7 MINUTES
SERVES: 4

CHICKEN SALAD

Yam kai

4 boned chicken breasts

garlic oil for brushing (see page 111)

some crisp lettuce leaves

5 scallions, chopped

½ cucumber, peeled and diced

¼ pound oyster mushrooms,
thinly sliced

¼ pound canned water chestnuts,
drained and sliced

For the dressing:

3 tablespoons *nam pla* (fish sauce)

juice of 2 limes

1 garlic clove, minced

2 teaspoons soft brown sugar

2 fresh red chiles, seeded and
cut into shreds

To garnish:

1 tablespoon chopped fresh cilantro

sliced red and green chiles

2 Arrange the lettuce leaves in a serving dish, and then sprinkle with the chopped scallions, diced cucumber, sliced oyster mushrooms, and water chestnuts.

1 Preheat the broiler. Place the chicken breasts on a broiler pan and brush liberally with garlic oil. Broil until cooked right through and golden-brown, turning once during cooking to brown both sides. Let cool while you prepare the salad.

PREPARATION: 15 MINUTES
COOKING: 20 MINUTES
SERVES: 4

3 Make the dressing: put the *nam pla*, lime juice, garlic, sugar, and shredded red chiles in a small saucepan. Place the pan over a low heat and cook very gently, stirring all the time until the sugar has dissolved. Remove from the heat.

4 Cut the cooked chicken into strips and arrange them on top of the salad. Cover with the warm dressing, and then garnish with chopped cilantro and sliced red and green chiles. Serve the salad warm.

CURRIED VEGETABLE SALAD

Nam prik deng Thai

2 sticks celery
4 carrots
¼ pound cabbage
¼ pound thin green beans
½ sweet red pepper
½ sweet green pepper
½ pound bean sprouts
½ pound canned water chestnuts, drained and sliced

For the curry dressing:

¼ pound creamed coconut (see page 111)
²/₃ cup water
2 tablespoons groundnut oil
2 tablespoons red curry paste (see page 111)
2 tablespoons dark soy sauce
juice of 1 lime
2 teaspoons brown sugar
¼ teaspoon salt
1 teaspoon ground cilantro
2 teaspoons ground cumin
3 tablespoons chopped roasted peanuts

To garnish:

few sprigs of fresh mint

1 Prepare the vegetables: coarsely chop the celery sticks into large pieces. Peel and slice the carrots thinly. Slice the cabbage, and trim the beans. Remove the seeds from the sweet peppers and dice the flesh.

2 Bring a large saucepan of water to the boil, and plunge in the prepared vegetables. Blanch them by boiling for 3–4 minutes. They should retain their fresh color and be slightly tender but still crisp. Drain and mix in a bowl with the bean sprouts and water chestnuts.

3 Make the curry dressing: put the creamed coconut in a bowl and cover with the water. Stir well until the coconut cream has completely dissolved, and set aside.

PREPARATION: 25 MINUTES
COOKING: 4–6 MINUTES
SERVES: 4–6

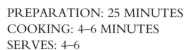

4 Heat the groundnut oil in a small wok or skillet. Add the red curry paste and stir well over a low heat for 1–2 minutes. Add the coconut cream, soy sauce, lime juice, sugar, salt, spices, and peanuts. Stir well and heat through gently for 3–4 minutes. Pour over the vegetables and toss gently. Transfer to a serving dish and serve warm garnished with sprigs of mint.

FRIED MIXED VEGETABLES

Bhud bhug raum mid

¼ pound cabbage

¼ pound cauliflower

¼ pound broccoli

2 carrots

¼ pound mushrooms

1 onion

3 tablespoons vegetable oil

1 garlic clove, minced

½ teaspoon freshly ground black pepper

2 tablespoons oyster sauce

⅔ cup chicken or
vegetable stock

2 ounces bean sprouts

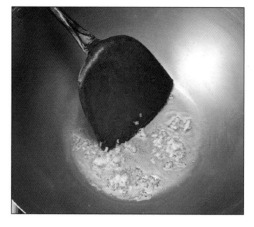

2 Heat the oil in a wok or deep skillet. Add the minced garlic and then stir-fry quickly over medium heat until golden. Do not allow it to get too brown.

3 Add the shredded cabbage and cauliflower florets, and a generous grinding of black pepper. Stir in the oyster sauce and the chicken or vegetable stock, and then cook, stirring constantly, for 3 minutes.

4 Add the broccoli, carrots, mushrooms, and onion to the wok together with the bean sprouts. Stir-fry for 2 minutes. Transfer the fried vegetables to a large dish or platter and serve immediately.

1 Shred the cabbage and separate the cauliflower florets. Trim and slice the broccoli. Scrape the carrots and cut into matchstick strips. Wipe the mushrooms on some paper towels and slice thinly. Peel and slice the onion into rings.

PREPARATION: 15 MINUTES
COOKING: 6–7 MINUTES
SERVES: 4

EGGPLANT WITH SHRIMP PASTE SAUCE

Nam prig bhug

1 Make the shrimp paste sauce: put the chopped garlic and red chiles in a mortar and then grind them until they are well blended and form a thick paste.

3 Cut the eggplants into thick slices. Put the beaten egg in a shallow bowl and dip the eggplant slices into it until they are all well coated with egg.

2 Transfer the garlic and chile paste to a small bowl and add the shrimp paste, lemon juice, sugar, *nam pla*, and ground dried shrimp. Mix well together until they are thoroughly combined. Set aside while you cook the eggplants.

PREPARATION: 15 MINUTES
COOKING: 5–10 MINUTES
SERVES: 4

3 small garlic cloves, chopped
4–5 small fresh red chiles, chopped
1 tablespoon shrimp paste
2 tablespoons lemon juice
1 tablespoon brown sugar
1/2 teaspoon *nam pla* (fish sauce)
1 teaspoon ground dried shrimp
3 eggplants
1 egg, beaten
oil for deep-frying

4 Heat the oil for deep-frying and fry the eggplant slices in batches until they are golden brown. Turn them once during cooking to brown both sides. Remove with a slotted spoon and drain on absorbent paper towels. Serve hot with the shrimp paste sauce.

STUFFED EGGPLANTS

Kayanthi hnat

1 Wash the eggplants and pat dry. Cut off the tops and scoop out the centers. Cut the scooped-out flesh into small dice. Season with a little salt and set aside. Fill the scooped-out shells with salted water and let stand for 3–4 minutes before emptying and rinsing the shells in fresh water.

24 small Thai eggplants
salt
2 ounces uncooked shrimp, shelled
¼ pound chicken breast, skinned and boned
1 scallion, finely chopped
4 garlic cloves, minced
1 tablespoon chile powder
1 teaspoon turmeric
1 tablespoon chopped fresh cilantro or parsley
2 tablespoons vegetable oil
1 egg
3 tablespoons cornstarch
3 tablespoons all-purpose flour
oil for deep-frying

To serve:

chile sauce (see page 110)

2 Chop the shrimp and chicken into small dice and place in a bowl. Add the scallion, garlic, and diced eggplant, and mix well. Season with chile powder, turmeric, and chopped cilantro or parsley. Bind the ingredients together with the vegetable oil, and season with extra salt. Knead to a smooth paste and use this mixture to fill the eggplants.

3 Make a thick batter: mix together the egg, cornstarch, and flour in a bowl, and add a little salt and cold water. Beat until smooth. Dip the filled eggplants into the batter so that they are thoroughly coated.

4 Heat the oil for deep-frying in a wok, large saucepan, or deep-fat fryer, and fry the eggplants, a few at a time, until crisp and golden brown all over. Remove with a slotted spoon and drain on absorbent paper towels. Serve with chile sauce.

PREPARATION: 30 MINUTES
COOKING: 7–10 MINUTES
SERVES: 4–6

STICKY RICE WITH MANGOES

Mamuang kuo nieo

3 Peel the mangoes and slice off the succulent yellow flesh by standing the mangoes upright and cutting down on either side of the stone. Cut the flesh into thin slices or "fans" with a sharp knife.

1 Soak the glutinous rice in cold water overnight. The following day, drain the rice and put it with the coconut milk, sugar, and salt in a large saucepan. Bring slowly to a boil, then reduce the heat and simmer gently until all the coconut milk has been absorbed by the rice. Stir the mixture occasionally.

2 Put the cooked rice in the top of a foil-lined steamer, and steam gently for 15–20 minutes over simmering water. Press the rice into an oiled cookie sheet, spreading it out flat and pressing down hard. Set aside until it is firm and thoroughly cooled. Cut the rice into slices or diamond shapes.

2 cups glutinous rice
2½ cups coconut milk (see page 111)
3 tablespoons sugar
pinch of salt
3 large ripe mangoes
To serve:
3 tablespoons palm or brown sugar
3 tablespoons water

PREPARATION: 20 MINUTES
COOKING: 35–40 MINUTES
SERVES: 6

4 Put the palm or brown sugar in a small saucepan with the water. Heat gently over low heat, stirring all the time, until the sugar is completely dissolved. Serve the rice slices or diamonds with the mango slices. Pour over a little of the sugar syrup.

COCONUT CREPES
Khan um kluk

2½ cups coconut milk

1 cup rice flour

3 eggs

½ cup sugar

1 cup desiccated coconut

pink and green food coloring

salt

oil for frying

To serve:

grated coconut

2 Divide the batter into 3 equal portions in 3 bowls. Color one pink, one green, and leave the other plain. Add a pinch of salt to each bowl and beat well. Let stand for at least 20 minutes.

3 Lightly oil a 6-inch omelet skillet and heat gently. When hot, pour in a thin layer of batter and, tilting the skillet, swirl it around to cover the base thinly. Cook over moderate heat until set and flecked with brown underneath. Flip over and cook the other side. Roll up the crêpe and slide on to a plate.

1 Make the batter: put the coconut milk, rice flour, eggs, and sugar in a large bowl and beat for 5 minutes. Fold the desiccated coconut into the batter.

4 Cook the remaining crêpes in the same way and keep warm. Stack the different colors in groups on a serving plate. Serve warm, scattered with grated coconut, with some fresh fruit.

PREPARATION: 15 MINUTES +
20 MINUTES STANDING TIME
COOKING: 15 MINUTES
SERVES: 6–8

FRIED COCONUT CAKES

Mok si kao

1 Put the sugar and water in a saucepan and heat gently, stirring all the time until the sugar dissolves. Bring to a boil, and then cook gently for 2–3 minutes, until slightly reduced and syrupy. Remove from the heat and set aside to cool.

2 Put the rice flour, egg, baking soda, salt, and coconut in a large mixing bowl. Mix all the ingredients together to a smooth paste.

PREPARATION: 20 MINUTES +
20 MINUTES STANDING
COOKING: 5–10 MINUTES
SERVES: 4

3 Pour in the cooled syrup and beat to make a smooth batter. Set aside for 20 minutes. Core the apples and cut into rings, and peel and slice the bananas. Add the fruit to the batter.

$\frac{1}{3}$ cup palm sugar or brown sugar
2 cups water
2$\frac{1}{2}$ cups rice flour
1 egg
2 teaspoons baking soda
pinch of salt
1 cup grated fresh or desiccated coconut
2 apples
2 bananas
oil for deep-frying

4 Heat the oil in a heavy saucepan, wok or deep-fat fryer, and drop in some large spoonfuls of the fruit batter. Fry in batches until golden brown on both sides, turning once. Remove and drain on absorbent paper towels. Serve hot with fresh fruit.

STICKY RICE WITH COCONUT MILK

Khow-nheaw moon

1 Wash the glutinous rice, cover with water and soak for at least 3 hours. Drain thoroughly and spread it out in the top of a large steamer. Place over boiling water and steam for 30–40 minutes.

2 Make the custard: combine all the ingredients in a mixing bowl and beat well with a hand-held whisk. Divide between 6–8 small basins or molds (or 4 coconut shells) and place in the top of one or two steamers.

PREPARATION: 40–50 MINUTES +
3 HOURS SOAKING
COOKING: 30 MINUTES
SERVES: 6

3 Place over boiling water and steam for 30 minutes, taking care that the water underneath does not boil dry. To test whether they are cooked, insert the point of a sharp knife into one of the custards—it should come out clean if they are cooked.

1 pound glutinous rice	
1³/4 cups coconut milk (see page 111)	
²/3 cup sugar	
1 tablespoon salt	
For the custard:	
6 eggs	
1 cup coconut milk	
²/3 cup granulated sugar	
¹/2 cup sugar	
1 teaspoon vanilla extract	
To serve:	
sliced mango	

4 While the custards are cooking, combine the coconut milk, sugar, and salt in a saucepan and bring to a boil over moderate heat, stirring constantly. When it boils, stir in the cooked rice, remove from the heat, and cover the pan. Let stand for 15 minutes. Serve with the turned-out custards and sliced mango.

SAUCES AND CURRY PASTES

CHILE SAUCE
Nam jeem

8 fresh red chiles, chopped
4 garlic cloves, minced
1 tablespoon *nam pla* (fish sauce)
2 teaspoons sugar
juice of 1 lime or lemon
1/4 teaspoon salt
1/2 cup water
2 tablespoons groundnut oil

Put the chiles, garlic, *nam pla*, sugar, lime, or lemon juice and the salt in a small saucepan. Stir in the water and oil. Bring to the boil, reduce the heat and simmer gently for 10–15 minutes. Blend until smooth in a food processor or blender. Store in a screwtop jar in the refrigerator for a maximum of 2 weeks. Use as required.

SHRIMP DIPPING SAUCE
Kapee khua

3 dried red chiles, seeded and soaked in boiling water until soft
2 tablespoons chopped lemon grass
6 shallots or 1 onion, finely chopped
3 tablespoons shrimp paste
2 ounces dried shrimp
1 1/4 cups coconut milk (see page 111)
1/2 cup ground pork
4 fresh red chiles
3 tablespoons palm or brown sugar
3 tablespoons *nam pla* (fish sauce)

Grind the soaked red chiles, lemon grass, shallots, and shrimp paste in a blender, food processor or mortar. Add the dried shrimp and grind to a smooth paste. Bring the coconut milk to a boil in a saucepan, lower the heat and simmer for 10 minutes. Add the ground chile paste and cook, stirring constantly, for 5 minutes. Add the ground pork and whole chiles, and cook, stirring, for 10 minutes. Stir in the sugar and *nam pla*. Serve with fried fish, shrimp, or vegetables.

THAI HOT SAUCE
Nam prik

2 tablespoons dried shrimp, soaked
3 teaspoons salt
1 teaspoon brown sugar
4 garlic cloves
6 anchovy fillets or 1 tablespoon salted anchovy essence
1 tablespoon soy sauce
4 fresh red chiles
lime juice

Put all the ingredients, except the lime juice, in a mortar and pound with a pestle to a smooth paste. Alternatively, whizz in a food processor or blender. Sprinkle with lime juice to taste and stir into the sauce. Store in a screwtop jar for up to 2 weeks. Serve with meat, vegetables, noodles, and rice dishes.

PLUM SAUCE
Num beuy

3 preserved plums plus 1 tablespoon liquid from the jar
2/3 cup water
6 tablespoons sugar

Put the plums, the plum liquid, and water in a saucepan and mix well together. Bring to a boil, and then boil for 1–2 minutes, stirring constantly with a wooden spoon to break up the plums. Press the mixture through a sieve and strain into the pan. Add the sugar, stirring well until dissolved, and bring back to the boil. Reduce the heat and simmer for 15 minutes, or until the sauce thickens and turns reddish in color. When cool, pour into a screwtop jar and store in the refrigerator.

GARLIC MIXTURE
Kra tium-prig tai

2 tablespoons minced garlic
2 tablespoons chopped cilantro root or stalks
1/2 tablespoon ground black pepper

This simple garlic mixture is a fundamental ingredient in Thai cooking and appears in many of the recipes in this book. Pound all the ingredients together in a mortar with a pestle until they are thoroughly blended and form a paste. If wished, it can be made in advance and stored, covered, in the refrigerator for 1–2 days until required. This will enhance the flavor.

GARLIC OIL
Num mun kra tium

4 tablespoons vegetable or sunflower oil
1 tablespoon minced garlic

Heat the oil in a small skillet and then add the minced garlic. Cook slowly over a gentle heat until the garlic is golden, stirring occasionally. Use in recipes as required.

RED CURRY PASTE
Kang bhed dang

6 dried red chiles
2 tablespoons chopped lemon grass
1 tablespoon chopped cilantro root or stalks
1 tablespoon chopped onion
1 tablespoon chopped garlic
1 teaspoon chopped galanga (khar root)
2 teaspoons cilantro seeds
1 teaspoon cumin seeds
6 white peppercorns
1 teaspoon salt
1 teaspoon shrimp paste

Scoop the seeds out of the chiles, and then soak them in cold water for 10 minutes. Drain well and chop coarsely. Put the chopped chiles in a blender or food processor and add the remaining ingredients. Process to a smooth paste. Alternatively, you can pound the mixture in a large mortar with a pestle. Store in a screwtop jar in the refrigerator for up to 3 weeks. Use as required.

GREEN CURRY PASTE

6 dried green chiles
3 tablespoons chopped scallions
1 tablespoon chopped garlic
1 tablespoon powdered lemon grass
1 tablespoon shrimp paste
1 teaspoon ground *laos*
1 teaspoon caraway seeds
2 teaspoons cilantro seeds
1 teaspoon finely grated lemon peel
1 teaspoon salt

Wash the chiles under running cold water. Remove the stalks and brush out any seeds. Put the chiles in a blender or food processor with the remaining ingredients and blend at high speed for 20–30 seconds, or until the mixture is a smooth paste. Alternatively, pound the mixture in a mortar with a pestle. Store in a small screwtop jar in the refrigerator for up to 3 weeks. Use as required.

COCONUT CREAM & MILK
Kati gon

3½ cups grated or desiccated coconut
3¾ cups milk

Mix the coconut and milk together in a saucepan. Bring to a boil, and then lower the heat and simmer, stirring occasionally, until the mixture is reduced by one-third. Strain, pressing the mixture against the sides of the strainer to extract as much liquid as possible. Pour the strained coconut milk into a bowl and chill in the refrigerator. When it is really cold, skim off the thicker "cream" that rises to the surface. The remaining liquid is the coconut milk.

TAMARIND WATER
Num som ma kharm

1 ounce tamarind
⅔ cups warm water

Wash the tamarind and leave it to soak in the warm water for 5–10 minutes; the longer you leave it to soak, the stronger the flavor. Squeeze out as much tamarind pulp as possible, and then press the thickened liquid through a strainer. Use immediately. If you wish to store the tamarind juice, you must strain it into a saucepan and bring to a boil. Remove from the heat and allow to cool in the pan before transferring the juice to a bowl. Cover and store in the refrigerator.

INDEX